Project Management

Project Management

the formal and informal approach

KARRAR SYED

PARTRIDGE

ISBN: Hardcover   978-1-4828-6395-6
             Softcover   978-1-4828-6393-2
             eBook   978-1-4828-6394-9

To order additional copies of this book, contact
Toll Free 800 101 2657 (Singapore)
Toll Free 1 800 81 7340 (Malaysia)
orders.singapore@partridgepublishing.com

www.partridgepublishing.com/singapore

Project management
The formal and informal way, success is guaranteed

Dedication

I dedicate this book to my mother the most practical and impressive Project Manager I have ever seen. And to my father who worked as a continuous support for the success of all the projects of life handled by my mother

I would like to express my most heartfelt and deepest gratitude to Mr. Ahmed Ramadan-Group CEO and chairman of Roya group, for being a portrayal of the true definition of a good leader and thus proving as an inspiration for me to be the same.

∞

Preface

I started my career from a Construction Company but I am unable to recall how I was attracted to interior fit out works. I remember, I joined a company involved in interior fit out works.

The job involved lot of coordination in terms of designing; and feasibility in the molding process. This gave me an insight into the human nature; our tendencies and habits.

The team working on the project communicated through designs and sketches.

I used to wonder, that in spite of receiving no formal education or training, the workers working on the project were completely aware of the intricacies of the design and that they also retained such a tremendous amount of confidence.

I stipulated that they must possess a talent that goes beyond the pages of a book.

We are constantly told that anybody that holds a high-level degree is in possession of endless knowledge. I pondered upon this, and finally decided to write a book that highlights and emphasizes on a practical approach towards Project Management. But, I ended up not being able to go beyond writing a few lines.

Hopefully, I will be able to write more elaborately on this subject in the future.

I started this book in 2011, but due to personal engagements, it was delayed. The structure of the book was changed many times before I finally stuck with the present one.

Initially, my mind was brimming with ideas and I thought I would be able to finish in a matter of months, but there came a point wherein I was unable to proceed.

I have been a keen observer of many things in my life, and here, I have tried to share few of my experiences.

Soon, my publisher began giving me reminders and deadlines.

Life itself is a project where not everything can be made note of.

I had promised to myself to finish the book by 2014, but that, due to certain circumstances, was not what happened; because some things remain out of our control.

It was on the 8th of January 2014 that my mother passed away. I could not bear the loss. I was shattered and was unable to think straight.

Suddenly, through my misery, I realized that I too was a project of my mother.

The relationship between a project and the project manager is exactly like a mother and her child.

I brought my father to live with us as he too was deeply affected by her passing away. He was happy among us, but his loneliness without her was unceasing.

He used to cry whenever he was alone. I realized that the success of any project is doomed unless a continuous support is in place.

My mother had supported my father unconditionally. But as I have mentioned before, that not all things remain in our control.

My father fell sick and stayed in the hospital for 52 days and on the 28th of May 2014, he too passed away. Now the situation was completely out of my hands. Life had come to the point where I was completely lost. I later gathered myself to write and complete the book, as this tragedy made me realize the real meaning of life.

Chapter 1

Book knowledge vs. practical knowledge

When we are children, we all have the same needs and aspirations, but what differentiates children in their growth, is mainly driven by the economic status they belong to. At this stage, their brains are fresh like a new sponge, allowing them to soak and absorb what ever they notice. They tend to accept it as an ultimate truth.

When they get a chance to play with mud, they start attempting to make different figures from their imagination and when they play with water, no time is ever enough. In cold countries, children play with ice, creating different shapes

1

and figures. Unknowingly, they are creating different projects.

In my opinion, our daily lives are nothing less than managing a project. Unknowingly we all do project management. Some are able to manage their projects better than others.

I want to share my thoughts about exercise. When we mature and get into a routine job, we realize the importance of exercising.

Although on a number of occasions I have joined a gym and hired full time trainers, or joined a yoga club, full of enthusiasm and determination, but as time passed, such activities began to become boring and wonderful people even initiated such a tedious activity.

Whenever I visit the doctor, his main prescription is always exercise. So a couple of months back, I once again started visiting the gym. But after a few months the usual problem started, I found it extremely boring and expensive; the hike in prices had started to burn a hole in my budget. Upon discussion, friends gave me varying opinions: Some would say to go for a daily walk, or get a family package to get a better bargain, and some were totally against the idea of joining a gym altogether.

With all this confusion, the only thing to do was to identify which opinion perfectly suited my requirement.

Once I realized the pivotal role of real requirement in decision making, half of my befuddlement had blown over because now I had an actual requirement and many reasons for joining the gym. When one knows where to go; the route has to be decided, that is, to pick the best suited option to your requirement.

Whether a job is done with the best possible results, in this case, depends entirely on you. Exercise contributes only 20% to a person's level of fitness. The remaining 80% is their diet.

Exercise alone may not help if the diet is not controlled. Whatever procedures I went through for joining the gym, the same process applies for any project however big or small the scale may be. This is part of project management.

On a daily basis, we are performing project management. Unknowingly, we use our skills in the form of application from dawn to dusk.

I have read this in one of the notes written by a mathematics professor, "the application of mathematics has actually given life to science, as I think that science is nothing but the application of mathematics as a tool to come to the conclusion". Arithmetic was discovered about 10,000 years ago and this started to help trading by being used for counting of money. Later the Arab world gave us algebra and it made trading easier. In every school, we are only taught to memorize formulas, prove theorems, and thus obtain a feeling of achievement. The actual *application* of mathematics is missing.

As human beings, we are capable of doing many things especially in today's world with so much of the information available at the touch of a button. How this has become possible, is application of knowledge which may be compared to connecting the dots. For example: Google started as a search engine, but has now become synonymous with all sorts of information like maps, books etc., it has slowly crept its way into our vocabulary. Today we say "When in doubt, Google it!" Google is no longer just a search engine. It has become a portal to sources of endless knowledge and information. Today a layman may become an expert on anything in a matter of days or hours, all due to Google. But there are other search engines, are theren't and just as big. Yahoo or Bing for example, how come one does not say "yahoo it or Bing it". This differentiation is all caused by the people driving these humongous projects. Both corporations may have the cream of software engineers, but it is the root of their expertise which makes the difference. Employees belonging to each respective enterprise may retain a similar amount of knowledge, but those of Google have the practical knowledge to apply it.

Practical knowledge, as is clear from the title itself, is attained by doing practical activities. It is the best way of achieving any goal. Nothing will happen by attaining knowledge based on merely the theories mentioned in a book.

In fact, if we look deeper, an institute prepares a person by providing him/her with applicable knowledge to perform in practical life. The performance of any good institute is directly related to the student's excellence in their practical battlefield.

Theoretical knowledge is very important, but, practical knowledge has a different level of importance. Like an automobile engineer designs an excellent car, but the actual worth of his work will only be recognized after the tires meet the road. And most importantly, its selling power.

Theoretical knowledge provides the proper understanding to perform better when a challenging situation arises.

When all the theory is applied practically to produce any kind of machine, the test run provides more input.

These inputs are in place due to practical knowledge and imagination. When one's imagination and the practical aspect of their intellect is combined together, we are able to obtain perfect results.

I want to share a real life situation

It was around 3:00pm in the afternoon; a time when everyone slows down due to fatigue or lethargy. The temperature outside was a whopping 48°Celsius and the project site was extremely hot and humid as air-conditioning installation was in progress. Everybody was sweating profusely at the site and yet the trade workers were working full of enthusiasm.

In this situation, various installation works were in progress, an engineer was giving instructions to the team, but the teams were not able to fully understand and the task was continuously being prolonged. Finally, the engineer requested the senior foreman on site to get the job done.

These kinds of problems are very common. Without the presence of practical knowledge, it is very difficult to sort out or carry out any task.

Even our subconscious works on practical applications of habit and behavior.

For example, if we just think of a green apple our mouth starts salivating, the brain never works based on theory, it is purely by experience. If we listen to our minds, our life would become a lot easier.

On a daily basis, an umpteen number of videos/ ideas are posted in the world of social media, but only a few watch and or take them seriously and try to implement these ideas in their lives.

Basically, the theories in those videos are easy to read. Their simplicity makes them easier to understand.

So the brain may store the information obtained by grasping only one aspect of action.

I had bought a computer from a friend, just to learn how to use one on my own, without asking anybody for help to avoid embarrassment. I had opened the computer in absolute privacy and then opened many programs and applications, but I had no idea how to use the commands.

Later, day by day, by trial and error, I learned the basic commands, all through practical use.

Even though many thorough and authorized books were available to learn the commands, I had learned them without need of purchasing these books.

If I would have gone through a book, the time taken for learning would have been extended, but practical approach shortened the time of learning.

At home one of the most technical places is the toilet flushing cistern. While doing the selection of plumbing items, we contact engineers and top line suppliers and visit their showrooms to select the best option based on the available budget. We then meet with the sales person, who explains the overall mechanism of operation. Convincingly we book the order and the material gets delivered to our homes. The final part is the installation. The installation stage requires a person who has experience in installing plumbing items to avoid any future complications and for the process to run smoothly. Why is a practical person required to complete this task? The qualification of that particular practical person is not necessarily checked. The bottom line is that the installation should be perfect.

Using the mantra of practice and practice, the practitioner learns the skill by experience, not only by reading and understanding.

Practical knowledge comes by experience. The experience registers in one's brain and finally in one's memory. Whereas just by learning through text book does not develop the skill as effectively.

In India the word jugaad (short cut) is very popular because the word jugaad is used to get anything running, specially mechanical or electrical machines.

This may be compared to one of my experiences.

Once we planned to travel by car for about 300 km to another city.

In the morning, we were all set to go. But when the car keys were turned, there was no roar of the engine. Someone else tried, and after their failure, everyone was soon attempting to start the car.

A friend, who was also a automobile engineer by profession, tried to find out the problem. It took him almost 2 hours to come to the conclusion that it was impossible to start the car.

So we decided to travel by train or bus. Someone suggested we should try one last time by consulting a nearby mechanic.

Eventually the mechanic came. The keys were handed over to him. He inserted the keys in and pushed a few buttons and just like that, the engine roared back to life.

Everyone was thrilled. We showed lot of respect and gratefulness to this practical person.

Then one of us asked what we were to do if we were to encounter a problem during the journey.

He suggested bringing the car to the garage for a quick fix (*jugaad*). So that we can enjoy the journey and upon returning we would repair the whole thing.

Prestigious project

An interior fit-out project was in full progress; basically it was a prestigious project for the company and for the project team. So everybody was full of enthusiasm and excitement, the team's focus unbreakable and with absolute concentration to avoid any kind of slippage. The duration of the project was around 2 years. This prolonged duration was due to exclusive items being used from around the world to enhance the ambience of the place and, at the same time, creating a work of art.

Experts from all around the world were hired to get the highest levels of expertise in order to meet the goals of the project.

The project team consisted of skilled artisans and connoisseurs who were intelligent enough to understand the pulse of the requirement.

In the beginning of the project many were deployed, only to be eliminated so that the cream of the cream remains.

So, at every stage of the project, members were cut off and finally 20 were chosen as apart in the final team.

Every stage of the project was monitored closely by means of joint inspection and immediate correction of errors. The tempo was very high in the first stage.

The ceiling design had been issued and moved around for approvals. After all the approvals, the contractor had been hired; he had gone through the drawing but could not understand it properly. Finally it was decided to create a prototype for the ceiling. The proto type was created, and it got approved.

Ceiling works started smoothly without any issues because the final product of the ceiling was clear to every team member.

Next, the flooring had to be finalized. The main issue was that the client sees only the mood board and some perspectives, but not the actual one. The translation of the client's requirement to the site or factory becomes of paramount importance. It is like the art of poetry, one word misplaced or changed in translation, the entire meaning would turn out to be a complete contrast to the actual requirement of the client.

The floor consisted of marble, mosaic, carpet and timber. The selected marble on board was 10x10cm, but the actual marble had veins.

So it was very important to install the marble, taking into consideration the minimization of the appearance of veins on the structure to ensure that it fitted the required theme.

The exercise for marble selection had started.

Instead of asking for a photo, everyone came to a consensus that it would be a lot better to see the actual finish.

We visited many marble yards to get the required finish, and finally got the required material. The marble was sorted. Now the next material to source out was the mosaic. The pattern of the mosaic was flowers and fish with many parallel joining curves joining along the marble.

The soft copy of the AutoCAD drawing was provided to the mosaic supplier as well as the marble supplier to avoid discrepancy in the dimensions. Both suppliers followed the same design.

In the meantime, the designer added one line of mosaic (size of the mosaic 25mmx25mm) in the outer periphery and this addition was conveyed to the marble supplier.

The marble supplier was a local, so they started early, and they went ahead and installed the marble all around the swimming pool and left space for mosaic wherever applicable.

It was a work in progress. The mosaic patterns arrived. We placed the mosaic, but, the interface line between the mosaic and marble was horrible.

In a few places, the interface line was matching but in most there were uneven gaps between the mosaic and marble.

We analyzed the situation and took action to sort out the issue and deliver the best quality to client.

We instructed the team to remove the marble which was in interface with the mosaic. Then we arranged the template to have a perfect and seamless line for the entire interface with the MDF.

It was more than five hundred pieces to fit in along the interface line. All the pieces were numbered.

LaterAutoCAD drawings were developed for the marble cutting and followed the same trick. The entire template converted into marble with coding like jigsaw puzzle. One by one they were installed and matched the perfect interface curve line. The flooring job turned out to exceed the expectations of the team.

It all happened due to practical approach taken towards the job.

Next, all other finishes were followed with soft furnishing items.

At every stage, a practical approach towards the job was the key element for getting the desired quality of work.

Because the project team was not trapped by the traditional theoretical approach but was instead given the liberty to be self-motivated, resulted in a job well done.

> ***Book knowledge is like loading a gun but practical knowledge is pulling the trigger***

Chapter 2

Project is the baby of project manager

Project management is a state of mind.

It requires a constant focus on the job. The first project manager in the universe is God almighty. The second is the team of the father and the mother. The mother is the real project manager taking care of different projects(read children) at different stages, whereas the father works as the initiator and support for the project's life cycle.

That's why normally the project has been termed as the baby of the project manager,

Here I want to focus on why it is always called a baby but a project manager never mentioned as the mother of the project. Simply because the mother has been termed as an ultimate choice for taking care of the baby. Similarly the Project manager is the ultimate choice for taking care of the project. So it is very important to understand the meaning of project manager. The project manager is simply like the mother of the baby. The project is the prime focus in the early stages where itis vulnerable, so it is the most important phase of the project. The project can be divided in 4 stages

1. start up
2. moving stage
3. maturity stage
4. final stage

Start up

Before the startup of any project, ground work is important and before anything else, The formulation of ideas for the project. If the idea stays for long, it begins taking shape.

A team is required which is capable to implement the idea as the idea converts into action. Nature supports the implementation of the idea. That's how a baby takes birth. If everything supports and moves in the favorable direction, the idea starts breathing in space and time. Once initiated, day by day it begins growing because *growth is nature.*

As time passes, the project grows. Building a project should not be the intention of the project manager. They should consider the project as their baby. When bringing up a baby, our main aim is that he or she must be capable of living and standing alone and performing well even in unfavorable conditions. For that the project manager must look at the project from all directions with a uniform dedication.

Moving stage

The start up phase provides all kind of tools to move the project. The movement of the project defines whether the start up phase is completely understood and taken care of.

The slightest negligence will reflect in the moving stage.

For some projects, even the movement is vulnerable because in the start up phase, the project manager might have neglected many important points. Certain points are irreparable, similar to any baby who if not well fed, can have effects on health all their life.

If the mother is immature, the grandmother or any other expert would provide her the knowledge to avoid any kind of ailment and ensure perfect health for the future.

Project structure also requires consultancies for the perfect health of the project.

Sometimes, when the mother lives with the baby all the time, it becomes difficult for a mother to realize developing symptoms, so they are pointed out to her by an expert such as an elder or a doctor.

Just as an expert visits and points out about any kind of abnormalities developed in the baby, in the same way, project meetings bring about the discussion and pointing out of any kind of abnormalities that may have developed and action is taken immediately to avoid any kind of damage to the project. This provides support to move the project in a normal way. The speed of the project directly depends on how well fed and taken care of the project is in the startup stage.

Maturity Stage

The maturity stage comes through the passage of time.

During this stage everything looks normal, and the project is moving. Sometimes at this stage the speed is slowed down due to certain other factors like weather conditions or the political situation, the road conditions, etc. These obstacles require an intelligent way to control the resources and spend in a more organized way to avoid scarcity of the resources. This is the stage of the project where more changes are possible. This is the place where most of the things are decided for the future. Usage of the facility or people or any product. This stage may be described as watchful and alert. It must be able to change suitably for the best product or project delivery.

I want to share an example

One of my relative's daughter was very good in her studies in the beginning of her junior classes. She was excellent in studies. The movement stage was excellent and as she entered into the maturity stage where all the line of expertise is decided she was admitted to the commerce side and she did well in commerce. Suddenly she got attracted to medical science. All her family was against this decision. But she started pursuing it. She studied again and appeared for medical entrance examination.

Finally she entered into the competition and she beat all the records of previous test and scored first position in the examination, the chief minister of the state honored her for the excellent performance in the examination and awarded her full scholarship. Likewise, project performance depends on the correct allocation of resource to get maximum potential effortlessly.

Final stage

The final stage of the project is exactly like handing over your grown up child to the world. The world starts scrutinizing every angle of the project. One loose screw will spoil everything. Likewise the behavior of the child reflects the guidance of mother.

The mother looks at the performance of the child. Successful project managers are those carrying out both good and bad projects, which provide knowledge for delivering the best project in every situation. Steve jobs had always picked all kinds of projects, good and bad both.

Suppose a mother has four kids and all are different in habits and in nature, she will be more worried about the one whose skills do not differentiate them from the crowd. Similarly, honesty towards the project is the key. The weak points of the project need to be identified and one must persist in correcting them. One of my project was in the final stage. The construction works were completed and the interior works were also going into the last stages. Each team member was fine tuning the project and making it ready for handover. The A/c was switched on finally, each member of the team was very happy about the project. Suddenly a foul smell spread all over the place the whole atmosphere changed.

Stopping the foul smell became the main task and all other activities took a back seat. The stink was unbearable. The ceiling services too were enquiring about the source of the smell.

One worker from with the working group mentioned that it could be coming from a dead cat.

Then everyone began searching all over and it became a big project to find the dead cat. But the fact that the space between the soffit and the false ceiling was little and it would be impossible for any cat to enter. Many temporary accesses were provided to access the ceiling to find the dead cat and finally the whole project had lots of temporary openings.

Cleaning works were carried out in the ceiling because many other issues were also found during the inspection like fire sealant was not properly done and that the MEP services were running haphazard above the ceiling. All these issues came to the lime light. Every highlighted point was to be closed and rectified, which delayed the project for 10 weeks.

So every stage of the project is very important and very important to follow the basic check list of requirements to avoid any kind of inconvenience in the next stage If the base is not done well nothing will be permanent and the entire project structure would collapse.

Chapter 3

Living around teachers

During our childhood, we have different perspectives, the first day in school is always difficult to recall because at that time we are in a different world. I remember only the head master of my school It was raining heavily and I had a colorful umbrella with three colors alternatively red, green and blue.

I kept an umbrella in the veranda outside, and later entered into the room of the head master, where he was sitting on a high back chair with a huge table in front of him. He got up from the chair, bursting with enthusiasm and offered me two toffees wrapped in colorful Aluminum foil.

I was very happy and excited about school. As of today, I still retain sweet memories about my head master. In junior classes, generally all the teachers shower love and affection as the children should find the environment welcoming and warm for their early basic learning.

We begin to mimic some teachers, walking like them, talking like them, wanting some part of them to be implemented within us, even if it's only putting on a tie and your dad's jacket. Sometimes the admiration we hold for them is to the point of fanaticism. We hold this untainted image of them as a beholder of ceaseless knowledge.

I remember one day, as many children who upon reaching home forget all aspects of the word "school", I forgot to do my homework.

The teacher asked the entire class to submit their homework. Everyone immediately opened their note books and proudly showed their homework to the teacher. Everyone except me. I was ashamed that day.

I had the bittersweet realization that this resulted from me not listening to my parents.

The teacher wrote a note, and asked me to show it to my parents. And so I did.

First things first, my mother and my father were polar opposites. My mother, lenient, and soft-spoken; and my father, an authoritative, uncompromising man. Using my wits, I showed it only to my mother.

It was my first note of complaint, so she was a little upset, and advised me to do my homework daily from the on. She said that this would gain me the love of the teacher and put me on top of the class.

This one lesson gave me the drive to achieve something, to make my mother proud, to gain the teacher's love, or as my mother had put it: to be on top of the class. I do not seem to be able to recall the grade in which I was in but this drive, this spark, desperate to **do** *something* was ignited.

From that day on, I was doing my homework regularly, displaying my diligence to the teacher every morning, bursting with accomplishment. Anticipating the red star to be inked into my notebook.

It was in 6th grade that we all had become very close to each other and it was on teacher's day we decorated the class room to show our respect and love for our teacher. Up until that time I had perceived the teacher as someone one seen in school but who belong to a different world. Someone who was a teacher by profession outside of school.

The life revolves around teachers and school. When we are in junior classes.. The world is an amazing place where we learn some things through guidance and then some by experience. I remember those days when my mamma was holding my hand to make an' A' and I would not concentrate.

But somehow I managed to start writing by the guidance of parents and my teachers. Now after passing 8th grade everybody feels like they have understood the world and that's why we all start arguing with people to convey the ideas endlessly boggling our minds. This is the stage which is very raw in terms of brain development. The development of brain takes place from the stage when we all first come into this world lying helplessly on the cot but downloading all the worldly information through the firing of neurons. Up to 5 years the partition between conscious and subconscious is not in place.

Up to 5 years whatever the information is downloaded into our brains. Later it becomes the part of the operating system. After 5 years the partition comes in place in between conscious and subconscious. Now no more down loading. This is why we often notice that the bright 5 years of kid becomes dull and less responsive after 5 years in terms of their performances and responses if proper moral support is not provided to the kid. Now after this stage and most of the time before this stage we are admitted to a school. We start learning in groups we look around and experience new things and the teacher/parent explains all kinds of curious observation made.

To start learning the secret code is practice, practice and practice That's why repetition takes the lead and is a proven method for good learning. Learning can also be done by observing our surroundings activities or learning by mistakes.

It was 5 o'clock in the evening I had gone to buy some stationary from a near by shop when I heard a person selling flutes. He did not shout to come and buy a flute. Instead he was playing a famous song. This song attracted many people to listen and some children were asking their parents to buy them a flute. I observed that instead of talking about the flute to persuade people to buying it. He adopted the method of direct experience of the product. Most of the Multinational use the same method. Now the question is whether

Multinationals have adopted their system or vice versa. Definitely Multinationals have adopted this by practical observation from surroundings.

Chapter 4

Unlearn to learn

The project manager has to be highly adaptive in terms of taking the responsibility of any project to finish and handover to the end user. One can understand it as a father's responsibilities at daughter's wedding. Each daughter is different and the father has to take care of her likes and dislikes

I was appointed as project manager for a company. The main activities of the company was cast gypsum ceiling works. As specialized contractor works under the main contractor, many times it happens that the contracting company adopts similar kind of system as the main contractor. I have learned the tricks to tackle the situation at site to get the all the work to be approved to the level of satisfaction to the main contractor and finally to the client. I became well versed with all kinds & site situations and became very confident in controlling the project.

Next job I was appointed as project manager from the main contractor side. Now this was a totally new role within the same working environment. All the tricks learned during previous job could not be possibly used. Now was the time that I had to unlearn whatever I had learnt, otherwise it would have been difficult to move and be effective in the new role. Project Manager from the main contractor's side is the main authority on site. The commander in chief of the project. The main driver of the project. Each and every activity has to go through the project manager.

Later I was appointed as project manager from client's side. Again whatever I had learned during the previous job became less useful because the approach towards looking at a project becomes different. The project manager from client side is totally different because at every stage of the project the client side project manager has to work like an expert. All the project activities are to be monitored according to the client requirement.

Recently I have completed a project where I worked as client's side project manager as well as subcontractor for the same job and main contractor for the same project. The situation was as below

Design and build a resort

The main contractor was appointed to carry the civil works(client representative Project Manager), Interior works was to be carried by the client's owned joinery factory(Subcontractor project Manager) the specialized works like glass and metal to be carried out from Client side (Main contractor) So I had to play all the three roles simultaneously. It was quite a tricky situation.

Chapter 5

The intellectual approach Vs application

Project Management principles

1-Understanding the importance of project management

2- Organizing for project management efficiency

3- Defining the roles of project manager and the team

4- Defining the roles of clients, customers and others

5- Setting up a planning and control system

1- Understanding the importance of project management

The importance of project management has been realized during high profile aerospace project such as Polaris and Apollo. During that period NASA and the US department of defence established project management standards. In the late 1960s to and early 1980 these standards provided lot of knowledge and support to the companies. Later these companies saw the potential benefits of formal project management. It has driven the whole working atmosphere into a well organized project.

Where large scale initiatives such as quality improvement and re-engineering provided data analysis and problem techniques. By 1990 the industries both profit and nonprofit organization realized that their operation will be unmanageable without adopting the project management techniques

Functional work versus project work

John was actually carrying out functional work like routine work as Quantity surveyor, but once the head of the department assigned him a specific function, He automatically became a project manager

John assigned a project – to manage engineer and manufacturing of a new product

John was asked – to develop a schedule as well as budget and present it to the executive management board within a week

Here I want to mention that by profession of John is a Quantity surveyor. The responsibility given to John for the engineer and manufacture of a new product which will bring the novelty in the market

John was asked to develop a schedule and budget, which is part of planning, to manage such a challenging task. He thought of following project management principles.

Project management principles to follow

- **Objective**– to have a better variety in the line of product range.
- **Program** – the program which estimates the cost of labor initially according to the concept of the product
- **Schedule** – the schedule states the WBS elements of a project, which includes Gantt chart, bar chart & the deliverables.
- **Budget** – the budget should be prepared based on the deliverables
- **Forecast**- the forecast of the delivery of the product should be done in accordance with the site situation and management policies

- **Organization-** the organizational structure which include the strategic management by launching new product, the organization to have executive management which will approve or reject, suggest for the successful completion of the product.
- **Policy** – a general guide for decision making and individual actions
- **Procedures** – the procedures to be made as guidelines for the organization to avoid confusion and polarization.

Roles and responsibilities of project manager

Functional mangers, including the managers of marketing, technology R&D, engineering manufacturing, material procurement, supplier management, customer suppot, sales, finance and quality, play a critical role in the success of any project. Their active participation and support to projects from the beginning to the end is crucial.

A project manager is responsible for the timely accomplishments of the objectives, team members as well as the methods applied.

- For successful completion of projects, project managers are required to assign create "correct alignment of team members that should work towards a common goal

- All the departments of an organization should work in harmony and provide correct inputs and outputs for completion of job on time.

- Project manager should be totally involved in all the tasks of the project in order to guide the subordinates to optimize their work.

- Being clear in distribution of responsibilities to motivate team members
- Proper Understanding of the project goal and understanding of the necessity of team work is most essential for the success of anyproject much more than paperwork.
- Proactive and practical approach to recognize the best method to achieve any goal.
- Minimizing and managing risk
- A project should be owned by a project manager. the project manager should understand objective, scope, deliverables and schedule of the project and thus manage its tasks
- Making sure that all the aspects of the project including the subcontracts given, if any, provisions of its statements of work (SOW) included in the plan of the project.

- Being open to ideas and suggestions of project team members motivates them, and ensures successful progress of the project.
- The project objectives should be achieved on schedule and within the specified budget
- Being the spokesperson for the project
  <u>John should take following steps to ensure the success of the proposed project.</u>

Conversion of a concept into an actual new product, the effort requires the resources and co ordination of all major stake holders, applying as much synergy as possible to solve common as well as unique team problems. Achieving a consensus on the product definition may be the most difficult problem to solve, since many solutions are usually available

The product planning process consists of several steps, an initial product concept development and testing marketing strategy development, business analysis, initial product development, test marketing and commercialization. The steps are not completely sequential, but overlapping, the initial product concept can be conceived at any time, even before the development of a new product corporate business strategy

However it should be remembered that new ideas do not always work out.

Those thought to be the most promising may, indeed be the most faulty, after all factors are considered. this is why many companies should have several new product teams working either in friendly competition or on projects related to a less tough development schedule due to a setting.

Introduction of any new product, the early planning would require sales forecasts to be completed before plans for manufacturing processes, industrial facilities, special tooling and marketing, could be developed. Sales promotions cannot be completed until the marketing research points in the direction for the promotions, performances and technical specifications as well as the many interdependencies among the production, marketing, finance, advertising and administration groups, must be resolved.

PRODUCT PLANNING:

Positioning of new products in the company structure

New products either have some fit with the firm's existing resources, including manufacturing, selling, engineering, technical service and purchasing or no fit at all. if there is no fit, the new product is really a new business investment, logic dictates that it should be run as a separate business if one runs it as a division, subsidiary or venture management problems often arise with regard to a product that does actually fit, which is the usual case. The best way to kill a new product, particularly in its early commercialization stage, it to put it under normal functional control.

Planning & cost control

Planning

Planning is determining what needs to be done, by whom and when, in order to fulfill one's assigned responsibility. There are nine major components of the planning phase

- Objective
- Program
- Schedule

- Budget
- Forecast
- Organization
- Policy – a general guide for decision making and individual actions
- Procedures& Standard

Cost control

Cost control is equally important to all companies, regadless of size, small companies generally have tighter monetary controls because the failure of even one project can put the company at risk. They have less sophisticated control techniques, large companies may have the luxury to spread project losses over several projects, whereas a small company cannot do the same.

The duties of business development also includes the coordination of a project or a new product from initial design through market availability.

In this capacity, they have no formal authority over either functional managers or functional employees. They act strictly on an informal basis to keep the project moving, give status report, and report on potential problems. They are also responsible for the selection of the plant that will be used to manufacture that product

What about John, is he qualified to uptake the challenge?

Selecting the project manager from Quantity surveying team will be more advantageous in completion of the task, with less changes and surprises because of the awareness of the project management in functional areas

Quantity surveying having functional expertise, so that the understanding part of the project can be reduced, the time will be saved to finish the project on time. The Quantity surveyor can identify the problems well in advance and take corrective actions.

Disadvantages

- The focus on the needs of the functional division might be difficult to see and respond to the needs of an organization as a whole
- Project control and status reporting to executive management is not a standard procedure and by doing this it will be difficult to manage the projects within the organization
- Project cost cannot be calculated accurately.
- The project manager is from a functional background so the project can become routine.
- The Quantity surveyor can work based on numbers but not in a political way

of controlling the project and keeping a balance among all the stake holders.

Role of project manager

- The role of a project manager is almost same as a leader. The project manager should induce the feeling of responsibility to the fellow team members like a sim card takes over a gadget.

- Integration skill – the project manager is the person working in all the places at all the stages of project. Right from objective, planning, execution and control. He/She is actually a link between all the co-ordination of aproject, other people working with limited boundaries and limited to their scope. A project manager carries forward the requirement of multiple trades in order to create harmony and feel good atmosphere for sharing the information between them.

- Technical skill – the project manager's competency also depends on the technical knowhow of the project. He should have expertise on the technical aspect the queries or the requirement that help in identifying potential problems

- Knowledge of organization – the failure of any project due to management problems will reflect directly on the inability of a project manager. The project manager should know the nature and personalities of people working in organization.

Part-2

Introduction-QUALITYMANAGEMENT CONCEPTS The project manager is responsible for quality management on the project. Quality management has equal priority with cost and schedule management. However, the direct measurement of quality is the responsibility of the quality assurance department for quality. From a project manager's perspective, there are six quality management concepts that should exist to support each and every project. They include:

- Quality policy
- Quality objectives
- Quality assurance
- Quality control
- Quality audit
- Quality program plan

Ideally, these six concepts should be embedded within the corporate culture.

Example

Project: Resort

Project manager: Mr. John

Scope of works: interior fit out works

Following methods used to quality assurance & quality control

Product inspection in factory

Explaining the required quality to various suppliers and installers

Quality check inspection by site supervisor

Direct communication from design office to site

Photographic inspection

Honesty towards the job

Visual inspection

Selection of product based on quality as well as the price tag

Giving more attention to interface details

Material storage

Managing hours of work

Listening to problems and trying to provide solutions.

Product inspection in factory

Advantages

It is generally observed that during the process of finalization of a contract to carry out the job, the suppliers put all efforts to get the contract. The submitted samples may be of higher quality as compared to their regular product. The factory inspection will make sure the received product is of the desired quality.

The factory inspection gives an opportunity to meet with different trade workers. Psychologically giving them the impression to that their work is going to be scrutinized at every step by a third party. The trade workers also try to improve quality on individual level

The factory has always followed quality methods for the process of manufacturing any product, which they supply to different clients. So during factory inspections we should respect their quality methods. We can ask for improvisations in quality which is good for both the parties.

The raw material used can be inspected, which is very important to achieve the highest quality of product.

Factory inspection gives quality control to the hands of the project manager instead of the suppliers.

Disadvantages

Generally factories don't like to be inspected. so when they get inspected, the entire factory starts to work in a different style to show professionalism in their working atmosphere, instead of thinking about the fact that the inspection is going to be carried out for their product and not their working style,.

Explaining the required quality to the supplier & installers

Advantages

Generally quality is achieved through the process of continuous improvement which is termed as total quality management, so to control the process, it is very important to explain the quality to all the trade workers and supervisor and those directly involved in carrying out the task. During the course of the process, the workers' mind will work in a guided direction, which helps in improving the quality of work.

While explaining the quality to the supplier and installers, it provides an opportunity to discuss the problems and finding possible solutions.

Disadvantages

No disadvantages

Quality check inspection by site supervisor

It can save a lot of time that would have been spent on making and remaking a product if the quality is checked by the site supervisor.

Disadvantages

Generally the site supervisor is responsible for the progress of work. Once the responsibility of quality is also given, the progress of work can be hampered.

The site supervisor works according to the general check list provided by the quality inspectors. This check list may not be fully compatible with the specific project requirement.

The term quality gives an impression to the site people that their work is going to be inspected by an authority, which creates an internal fear of failure; this leads them to follow the old traditional rules in their working style instead of working on their own based on their own experience.

Direct communication between design office and site

Advantages

The communication in terms of drawing and details is the most important point in achieving required quality. This helps in making the site work up-to-date with the revised drawings and details, if any, on time and saves demolition/modification of completed work.

Disadvantages

The design office has an advantage by having direct contact with the site to conceal their problems, which they might have not considered in the drawings & details. When they walk on site they realize the missing details of the design or approved workshop drawings. The contractor suffers because of the direct involvement of design office to the site.

Photographic inspection

Advantages

Photographic inspection is very useful to achieve quality. The progress photographs help in monitoring the site work from the office.

It has been noticed many times that certain things can be overlooked at site. As what we see and realize is all based on the attention we give. We see what we want to see. But in the case of a camera by zooming the image, each and every detail can be inspected, and immediate action can be taken to avoid any problems in future.

Disadvantages

No disadvantages

Honesty towards the job

Advantages

Honesty is the best policy; honesty towards the job is a very important aspect to achieve high quality. Site work also requires honesty to achieve quality, because honesty leads to purity and achievement for any kind of job.

Honesty towards the job is essential in order to reduce quality checks; if the team members are honest the job will be completed with excellence.

Disadvantages

No disadvantages

Visual inspection rather measured

Advantages

Visual inspection is preferred because it involves looking in totality instead of any particular item.

It gives a broad vision of looking into the quality of work

Disadvantages

Visual inspection does not have any records in terms of quality procedures, which may create a lot of confusion and conflicts related to drawing and details.

Purchasing policy (Selection of product based on quality instead of the price tag)

Advantages

The selection of product must be based on the quality because the selected product will become part of the project, if the selection is based on quality and suitability rather than the price tag only, the quality of the entire project is improved.

Disadvantages

Generally the selection of any product is based on price tag to keep the budget of the project under control. Sometimes suppliers take advantage by raising prices unreasonably.

(Detailing)Giving more attention to interface details

Advantages

1. The interface details are the most important aspect to achieve the quality of the project. For an example; if two different elements are installed together without considering their properties, they may lead to warping and twisting of the details after a certain period of time due to change in temperature. The beauty of the product lies in the detailing

of the interface, and considering the properties of materials according to the details provided.

Material storage

Advantages

1. The storage of material is also one of the paramount aspects to achieve good quality. If the storage of material is not as specified by the supplier it may lead to material damage.

Disadvantage

No disadvantages

Avoiding limited working hours

Advantages

Trade workers are like artists so they require concentration and liberty. If one works with a free mind the quality will definitely improve. This is why old structures have stunning designs & details. Even to this day no improvisation is required.

Disadvantages

The present era does not allow the trade workers to have unlimited working hours, and all projects are controlled by a set budget and time frame, resulting in not being able to give enough time and money to achieve excellent quality.

Listening to the problems and providing solutions

Advantages

1. Quality is achieved by continuous improvement, which may only be done by identifying the problems. The solution can be achieved by listening to practical problems faced by trade workers.

Conclusion

According to the literature written for TQM; there is no proper definition of total quality management. Some professionals define it as providing the customers with quality products at the right time and at the right place. Others define it as meeting or exceeding customer requirements. Internally, TQM can be defined as continuous improvement in the quality of the product and less waste. Finally the project manager is the one responsible for the quality of the project. This is true for the same reason that the top management of the company is ultimately responsible for quality in a company. The project manager should have the liberty to select the procedures and policies for the project and therefore controls the quality. The project manager must create an environment that builds trust and cooperation among the team members. The project manager must support the identification and reporting of problems by team members to improvise the overall quality of the project

Quality leadership is an alternative that emphasizes results by working on methods. In this type of management, every work process is thoroughly studied and continuously improved so that the final product or project not only meets but exceeds customer expectations. The principles of quality leadership are customer focus, obsession with quality, effective work structure, control yet freedom (e.g., management in control of employees yet freedom given to employees), unity of purpose, process defect identification, teamwork, and education

<u>Valuable advice for adopting ERP system</u>

Organizations normally function based on systems made by the higher management and the communications made through outlook express between different departments internally.

The accounts department has to work with the technical department for recording financial transactions, so each department is solely dependent on each other to run the organization smoothly. If one department is not providing the reports or updating on time, the whole organization comes to a stand still.

The adoption of ERP system is the only solution to integrate all parts of the company seamlessly. By doing this, a higher degree of control is possible. ERP systems are able to minimize redundant data registration and reduce registration errors.

The interconnectivity among all the modules of ERP systems drastically reduces the time period to perform different operational tasks, which directly increases the efficiency of the company. The following are the main reasons to adopt ERP systems.

1. To integrate financial information
2. To integrate customer order information
3. To standardize and speed up manufacturing processes.
4. To standardize inventory
5. To standardize HR information

6. To standardize supply chain management

7. To standardize project management system

Each department personnel may act independently. They don't have to consult the related department every time to record financial transactions.

It ensures quicker processing of information and reduces the burden of paper work

It serves the customers more efficiently by way of immediate response and taking action.

It helps in having a say over your competitor and adapting to the whims and fancies of market and business fluctuations.

The data base becomes user friendly and it also helps to do away with unwanted ambiguity.

ERP is best suited for global operations as it covers all the domestic meaningless talks, currency conversions and multilingual facilities, in short, *think local act global.*

Reasons to not adopt ERP systems

The ERP system is mainly initiated in a certain type of industry but may not suit all kinds of businesses; the modern enterprise resource planning systems have their roots in material requirement planning systems, which were introduced in the 1960s

So right now the ERP systems are best suited for the manufacturing industry, where production, storage, delivery and customer satisfaction is involved. Later it may be developed to suit all types of industries. Even advanced times ERP system implementation is a challenge for both vendor and client so that the organization may take full advantage of the ERP system.

The ERP system is rendering marvelous services but it also has its own limitations. Primarily ERP calls for exorbitant investment in sense of time and money. The amount of money required to implement the ERP system will not guarantee benefits, but is subject to proper implementation, training and use. It is alarming to note the time taken to implement the system in any organization. This means large amount of workers have to compromise on the regular working hours and undertake training, this not only disturbs the regular functioning of the organization but also runs the high risk of losing potential business during that particular period. ERP system is like cement, in the beginning, it looks very flexible, but later it is very difficult to change.

Risk in consideration while adopting ERP

For implementing the ERP

It is very common fact that the ERP implementation is not the only solution for the integration of all data at one common database, accessible to the required department.

The implementation of ERP has risk factors which also must be considered while implementing ERP system.

I have worked in a company where the ERP had been implemented for two years but still we faced problems in carrying out tasks by fully depending on ERP.

My company had the following departments

1. design department
2. interiors department

3. transport department
4. facility management department
5. technical department (Construction, Landscape)
6. procurement department
7. material handling and logistics
8. real estate department
9. events management department
10. project management department
11. finance department
12. human resource department

ERP had been implemented for the smooth functioning of all these departments, but we still faced problems. The interior products had a wide variety and ranges available with different suppliers all over the world; every product completely different from the other because of the difference between the clients and nature of use.

So every time a new coding for each material must be created and only then can the purchase requisition be created, but without ERP it becomes easier to create a purchase requisition by providing full details of the product instead of a code in the purchase requisition.

The other problem was usage of the project return materials (returned due to change of mind by the client or by designer), which had been stored under the material handling & logistics department for future use. If an item to be used was from some other project's stock to receive the allotted item, material reservation was needed to be made and then had to be approved in the system. Approving and creating the budget was not linked, so, if the budget was not uploaded during this procedure andinstead was uploaded while arranging the delivery of that reserved item to the site, the system took the budget into consideration. Thus generally we bypassed the ERP due to urgency of the project.

While creating the material reservation the budget should be connected, so the budget issue may be overcome in the beginning to avoid any last minute surprises.

Mainly the finance department benefits the most with the ERP implementation and other departments do not as for them phone calls and face to face communications become necessary to complete any task

Some risk factors must also be considered whilst implementing ERP

- Single point of failure
- Loose security policies
- support protection
- Limitation of technology
- False sense of security

- Weak encryption
- Latency risks

However, an interesting finding here is that the progress of ERP implementation project has no impact on the benefits of ERP even though it is correlated with ERP benefits. This indicates that although an ERP implementation project was not completed on time and within budget, a company still has a chance to get the full benefits from the ERP system if its quality and scope is satisfactory.

The best case scenario is if an implementation project is completed on time, within budget, with good quality and matches the scope. But realistically, this may not always be the case.

If the progress of the ERP project is good, but the quality is bad, it will eventually fail because users may be reluctant to use it. If both progress and quality of the project are bad, it will be abandoned, even before the system is materialized. Therefore, to minimize the risk of ERP implementation, we should focus more on improving the quality and scope of the ERP system rather than the progress of the ERP project.

More factors to be considered while implementing ERP system

1. During the implementation of ERP, a negative approach may also be effective to a degree because the organization works on a previously existing system; a system which was developed based on the experiences within the organization.
2. Transferring data from the existing system into a new system is a challenge. It may lead to years' worth of backlog resurfacing.

During this process, the upper most tier of management may also get involved due to the considerable amount of money and time involved. At one point the whole organization becomes extremely sensitive so it is very important that the top management realizes the situation in advance to build up confidence within the organization in order to ensure thatthe benefits of the ERP system is felt by each individual of the organization.

3. Once each individual worker attains confidence in the new system, useful information will be provided proactively. Data transfer and other related information will be tailer-made to the ERP system.

4. The success of ERP implementation will owe to the success of the entire organization.

Due to the fact that the implementation of the ERP system takes a prolonged period of time for implementation, it results in the development of relationships between the vendor team and each key, responsible person within the organization. It becomes a common goal to make the new ERP system asuccess.

5.   The functions of the ERP system should be well defined to cover the company's necessary business functions. It is also important to choose the right software considering whether or not it can support the defined functions as well as its functionality.

6.   All the members in the company should be encouraged to use the ERP system because their use can increase the company's business value.

7. To make the ERP system more useful, the company should focus more on enhancing the quality of output during its implementation, especially in regard to the management reports and measurement reports.

8. The ERP system should be easy to use. A complex system decreases its usefulness, which also make users reluctant to use it. The system should be carefully designed to be user friendly, considering screen design, user interface, page layout, help facilities, menus, etc.

9. The company should clearly define what positive results are expected from the use of the implementation of the ERP system. This can make the system more useful, and help users to understand why they should use the ERP system.

10. To maximize ERP benefits the company should focus more on the quality and

scope of the ERP system matching with the company's needs. To achieve this, well defined functions, as well as the right software, is mandatory.

11. The company should clearly define what positive results can be expected from the use of the ERP system before or during ERP implementation. This can make the system more useful, and help users understand why they should use the ERP system

Conclusion

The ERP system implementation should be aimed to be done in minimum time. Because of the length of the time required for its implementation, organizations are sometimes discouraged to adopt it.

Local and small vendors get better ratings than global vendors due to the satisfaction level between varying aspects. All in all, it depends on how the project management and system design have been implemented

Excellence in project management

Adoption of Prince2

Present Situation of the Company

The following are the major activities of the company

- **Project management department (PMD)** – The PM works as an individual unit and act as the client representative of the project. The information flows from this department to other departments.
- **Design department** – Based on the briefings provided by the PMD, the design proposals are made and sent for approval to the client through them. The designs may be approved for structural

works, but the interior design proposal may be rejected and the designer has to once again take briefs from the client to avoid further rejections.

- **Interiors department** – The interiors department works on the design and details provided by the design department in co-ordination with the PMD representative.

- **Landscaping department** – The landscape department also works based on the details and design provided by the design department.

- **Transport department** – The transport department works to fulfill all the transportation needs of the entire company.

- **Construction department** – The construction department works based on the drawing and details provided by the design department.

- **Material handling department** – The material handling department works along with the procurement department.
- **Procurement department** – The procurement department works in co-ordination with all departments to procure all the required material for the project.

The project demands the integration and cohesion of all departments. To carry out projects in the best way possible, adopting prince-2 will be the best option due to the following points:

Advice in Making Decisions

The first and the foremost important point for adopting prince-2 is that it works in a controlled environment and every stage of the project recorded. Much before the starting of a project, the business case becomes the prime factor, which explains all details in terms of all the possible information related to why a project is to be carried out.

The following questions should be asked to analyze the nature of the project:

What is to be achieved?

Why does it need to be done?

How will it be done?

Who needs to be involved?

How long will the work take?

How much will it cost?

What additional resources are needed?

The above questions should be asked by the work group to clarify the concept and idea behind the project and also to create the overall strategy to run the job.

Advantages of adopting prince-2 methodology:

Before the introduction of any new methodology the reason for its adoption is always questioned. It is important to have knowledge of how the company is managing projects without prince-2, and what problems are faced during the life cycle of the project.

Reasons for Project Failure

Below are listed the common reasons for project failure

1. Responsibilities and leadership roles are not clear
2. Lack of understanding and undertaking of the project.
3. Lack of details of quality requirement and acceptance criteria- for example, a project is completely based on the

specifications and details, but after completion, the inspection team starts finding faults without providing the acceptance criteria prior to start of the project.

4. Due to the fact that the user /client are not involved or over involved at each step, there can be more chances of facing sudden changes and rejections.

5. As it is often said that *"50% of project management is to manage the changes while the project is in progress"*.

6. The specification of the project is poorly specified and it results in the client being handed over a misinterpreted and unsatisfying project.

7. The final goal of the project is not defined at the beginning of the project.

By considering the above, failure of any project may be avoided. By implementing a project management system which works in a controlled environment all the loose ends will be tied-up at project closure.

So it is very clear that PRINCE-2 is the only methodology of project management which has been developed to work in a controlled environment, where each stage of the project is measured. *"And it teaches how to do project management practically"*.

"The beauty of Prince2 is: it can be applied to any project; and it is not a rigid methodology, it can be tailored to suit the parameters of the project"

Methodology of Prince 2

Before adopting prince-2 we should know about the methodology and how it works. The prince -2 methodology works in a very simple way of working, though it gives the best possible solutions to complex problems.

The body of any project has three parts: start, middle and end. To start with, the prince -2 contains the following eight components and principles

1. **Business case** – the business case identifies the clear cut idea of the project. It also defines the details of the product benefits in terms of usage and achieving the main goal of the project

2. **Plan** – once the business case has been approved by all the stakeholders, the planning is the next step. It analyses the job in terms of looking into the actual product, the plant equipments and resources.

3. **Organization** – now it is the time to identify who is going to use the product, the client or/and the customers, so it is important to have a discussion about testing and commissioning.

Furthermore, Responsibilities must be delegated.

4. **Risk** – the risks need to be identified and accordingly managed, based on the type of risk involved, as every product has a different type of risk involved.

5. **Change** – the client might be busy doing other things but it is important to provide information during the progress of the project, because the decision processes of all the stakeholders are mandatory. So at every stage of the project, a thorough decision process is required.

   It may be that the client has a different perspective on certain information.

6. **Change control** – When a client requests any changes in the specifications earlier provided, it becomes important to take them into consideration. At the same

time, the budget and time constraints should also be accounted for.

If any revisions are to be done, in prince-2 every stage of the project is recorded and each stage of the project has clear cut decision procedures.

7. **Configuration   management** –configuration management is one of the most important parts of prince-2. if the client has changed the size of or color or shape of any particular product, it is the responsibility of configuration management team to ensure that the change has been incorporated in the system. Based on this change, the information is forwarded; performance of configuration management can be identified by the number of faults reported during the project's life cycle.

8. **Managing stage boundaries-** the most important part of prince 2 is to

manage stage boundaries. This has to be managed by the project manager at every stage of the project. A project should be taken to the next stage once the previous stage is approved by the client/stakeholders.

Steps to take into Consideration before adopting Prince2

The present system of working should be taken into consideration and the system of Prince-2 should be superimposed. By doing this exercise, we shall know if any previous system of working matches at any point or stage of workflow. Once it is identified, the strategy can be formed as prince 2 works in a controlled environment.

It defines the clear authority and responsibility of all the stake holders. So it becomes very important for all the stakeholders to participate actively otherwise the system will not work.

The organization should have the capability to work in a way that is professional to achieve the best possible results within the available resources. For adopting the new system, the working environment must be upgraded to achieve the best possible results.

The highest level of management is the most important stakeholder in the decision of adopting Prince- 2, because the decision process is purely professional.

If the highest level of management has too many people, then it becomes important to delegate an individual who will be totally responsible for Prince-2. They will assign the responsibilities as per the requirement for the adoption of Prince-2

The most important department of the organization is that of Project management because this department is responsible for taking briefings from the client. If we compare with the prince 2 methodology, the business case will be prepared based on the brief, so it becomes important to hire a professional well versed with business case proposals.

The second most important department is the design department; this department is responsible for creating the design and details of the product, which are one of the most crucial aspects of a project. The briefing may not be enough to meet the client requirements. This may result in rejection of the product.

To achieve the best results and attain maximum benefits from the adoption of any methodology, it is always important to prepare all the members of the organization in such a way that they fully understand its welfare to the company. This way communication will be fast and effective.

Before adopting any methodology research is very important to understand the requirement of the professionals.

It has been found, on many occasions, that human error gives a way to develop a system to avoid these errors and achieve the maximum output with minimum effort.

Before adopting a system, the preparation is the most important part to achieve the best possible results.

For example, if we want to prepare a mold, before making the mold the exact piece has to be prepared with respect to all the dimensions and details so it becomes important that before making the mold the product information has to be taken into consideration. More time will be consumed in making the mother piece. The mother piece is to be considered like the organization and the prince 2 is to be considered as the mother mold. To get the best results, the mother piece must match the mother mold, taking the maximum welfare from the system.

Conclusion

Adopting Prince-2 can surely prove advantageous for any organization; providing all the members of that organization are well prepared and trained before its introduction.

Apart from the above the two stages, closing of project and Quality review technique will be developed during the adoption of Prince -2.

Chapter 6

The illusion

Illusion by definition is distortion of senses Everything around us is an illusion. Nothing is what it seems. Our senses are translating and providing information to the brain and the image appears. The colors that we see may not be real. In actuality they may be a translation of a private interpretation of our mind. But our daily life is based on our collective consciousness. Humans are the one of the only species able to distinguish between colors around us. The beautiful birds that we enjoy keeping as pets for their extravagant appearance do not know the reason why humans admire them. Each being experiences this world differently. The senses of each species are wired differently. How a bird perceives a dog we do not know. The world around us is magical, in which, as aforementioned, nothing is what it seems.

Our senses are limited, we can't hear more than 20,000db and less than 20dbs and we can't see less than 7 micron.

In a nutshell, we are living in an illusion all the time.

When we talk, we hear, but we really are just sensing vibrations in the air and these vibrations travel to the hair in our ears called cilia and translates into sound. All the five senses we use are based on one soul sense which is the *knowing sense*. Without it no other sense would function.

Humans can't see the same way in both air and other mediums as the hawk can see 8 times better than human eye medium with no variation in the amount of precision. It is due to this sensory speciality that hawks are able to catch prey by diving towards the ground from the air in one shot.

Making someone's dream a reality

You are not your brain. In fact the brain is like a tool we use to live happily in this world. But sometimes, it may take over control of you. It does this by obstructing any kind of information which may be perceived by you differently. To be able to handle and account for this illusionary deficit is a very important part of project management. The project manager sees and looks at things differently. The project is awarded, the project manager appears to be the pivot for all the activities required to complete the job.

For example, if you have a servant at home and you are the head of the family, their quality of work and diligence will be based on your behavior towards them. If you are absolutely no-nonsense and reprimanding, things will be in much more in control.

Suppose if you give them the liberty to work on his accord; he will bypass you and after a period of time, he may represent himself as your avatar when a situations arises. He would go out of control. Your brain also works in the same way. We should try to identify ourselves. Who is living all over our body besides in ourhead?

"The brain is a terrible master and a wonderful servant". By Robin sharma

In our daily life, we face the illusion of professional defiance, that is, the belief in the absolute perfection of every individual who specializes in a particular area; that this individual has no margin of error. This is not true.

We are living in ecosystem. The balance of this ecosystem is maintained by all its residents; each individual assigned varying responsibility to maintain that balance.

In an interior fit out project, the Client depends on the designer; the designer on the project manager, and finally the project manager on his team. Most of the time if each entity works separately the work will never finish.

Most of the time, the project manager possesses more knowledge and has more exposure than the designer. In this case, the Project manager provides support in terms of design. This becomes technically viable in installation due to mutual knowledge sharing.

As per my experience, the designer (major interior designers) retains the knowledge, but the practical entity of an idea remains intangible. These types of designers normally conceal the missing element to their idea and try to get the information by providing half hearted details and searching for the other half with the project team. Then, the concept of the design is translated to paper. However, this transition may not always be smooth sailing and there may be mistranslations of ideas/concepts along the way, resulting in the project team being misled and there being wastage of resources.

An example:

The designer designed a lobby with big arches and columns with very intricate detailing but had not emphasized on the column capital. After everything has been built up, it looks very impressive in all aspects except the column capital. The column capital is not in line with the overall design; and, being on eye level, it immediately became the prime focus of the project team.

The client, upon viewing the lobby, complained about the column capital and accordingly, the designer started working on its design; ultimately coming to no sort of conclusive direction to move in for the column capital.

In this case, one may say that the illusion of client was not understood by the designer to properly manage it and bring it to life.

Then, the entire team began looking for inspiration through Google and finally, an image was selected to show to the client. The designer pasted the 1:1 photo of the capital on exact location.

We were all collectively having a different illusion so we all approved of it and confidently showed it to the client. The client agreed to proceed with the mock up. The mock up works started based on the precise design shown in the photograph. The mock was made ready for further inspection.

Then, we all realized that the capital was large in comparison to the column and other elements in its surrounding.

It all happened because of difference in visualization of the elements.

Now from our project team, a senior construction manager has took up management of the illusion of the client and he began working on some base design which was previously approved by the client. He discussed it in great detail with the client to fully translate it into words, ensuring complete capture of the image in the client's mind.

He then started drawing up the design in collaboration with another draughtsman. Then this image was discussed with the entire team so as to confidently in the direction of his understanding of the client's illusion.

The client somehow agreed to the drawing to precede with the production of 3-d model, during the production of 3-d model many more changes taken in place because the image became clearer. Before completing the 3-d model it was decided to take the client along to see the 3-d model under process just to make sure of whether we were on the same page. The client visited the place and requested to change the base lines and the proportion of some design elements. It happens because what we see from our eyes is not the same as another person looking at the same time and the same place. It is our focus which makes lot of difference, we see what we focus on rest is just filling of gap.

When we really focused on the element, in this case, the capital came out approximately as imagined by the client.

Chapter 7

Living examples

Undulations in gypsum ceiling

I was the in charge of gypsum false ceiling for an airport project; the size of the project was big in terms of the values and area. The false ceilings always gets delayed and thus have the shortest time period before submission of the project. This happens because all the other above ceiling works require a much longer period of time and their works run through most of the project. The project had been going on for 2 years and it was observed by the entire team that everybody's gaze first falls upon the ceiling finish than any other finish. Once the ceiling is finished the project will be completed in the eyes of client, but, the undulation was visible in the ceiling in many places. A special team was formed and the task was to complete all the visible ceiling undulations within 2 days for the whole area. The target was seemingly unrealistic; 12,000 square feet of ceiling to be done up in 2 days. But we did not have a choice.

The whole ceiling was divided into 8 typical bays.

But, when the ceiling lights were switched on, all the undulations visibly, ceased to exist. We offered to have the ceiling inspected the very next day; It was a straightforward approval, no comments made. Although it was only due to the lights that the ceiling seemed flawless, this did not prove to be a problem as the lights were to be always on due to the fact that it was an airport. Sometimes we forget to check the finishes the actual conditions of the finished project.

SMART SELECTION OF CEILING LIGHT RESOLVES THE FINISHING PROBLEMS OF THE FALSE CEILING

Demolition of an old villa

I was part of a project to demolish an existing villa shifting all the items into the new facility. Our team gathered and adopted a demolition plan to ensure that each and every item was shifted. 5 teams were assigned as below to carry out the task with a guarantee of completion and safe handover.

- Furniture items
- crockery items
- decorative accessories
- soft furnishings
- miscellaneous items including pets

Furniture items - All the furniture were inspected and properly tagged with the item number and photo for easy reference, items were then packed and shifted

Crockery items - All the crockery items were thoroughly inspected; each item packed in bubble wrap and tagged with an item number and picture and then packed separately as sets and then in bigger cartons for easy handling and shifting.

Decorative accessories

All the decorative accessories were inspected and tagged accordingly with the appropriate item number and picture to visualize the item inside the box. Then they were properly packed in cartons with thermocol chips for safe handling and shifting.

Soft furnishings

All the curtains bed linens and other soft furnishing items were properly removed and packed well with a color code and wherever possible, an attached specification sheet with the photograph of the item to provide proper details without opening the pack

Miscellaneous items and pets

The items which cannot be done without such as housekeeping items, shelving units, and house pets were given to the responsibility of the caretaker because he knows the necessity and proper handling of these items, as well as the fact that he was the main keeper of the client's dogs. The caretaker took the responsibility to take care of the assigned task.

All the items were shifted to the assigned warehouse for future use except the Pet dogs.

The pet dogs (Rottweiler) were sent to a nearby kennel.

The demolition project was successful in terms of shifting and proper storage of valuable items.

After one week the client called our director to send the dogs into their new home. Director confidently said that he would send the pets immediately. He then called his assistant to pick them up from the kennel and hand them over to the client immediately.

After about an hour the client called once again. The Director assumed that he had received his pets and this may be him thanking him. He answered the call with a relaxed tone.

On the other side of the line was a voice filled with agitation. As his voice boomed through the speaker, the client asked why he still had not received his pets. The director was furious.

He called the assistant to know the status. The reply he received was shocking.

The Assistant informed him that he was at kennel and that there were about 50 Rottweiler's and he had no idea how to identify those that belonged to the client. The director asked him, still enraged at his incompetence, why he hadn't called the caretaker who would identify them immediately. The assistant replied with the excuse that he was on leave in India.

The director then asked him to just call him, only to later hear that he did not have any means of cellular communication as he resided in a remote area; the address of which the assistant had. By this time, the Director almost fainted, because he had received more than 50 calls from the client asking about his dogs.

The Director left everything and asked the assistant to meet him at the airport with the home address in hand. Both the assistant and the director followed up the address and took the flight to India. After reaching there, they enquired about how they would reach the place and finally, one cab driver agreed to take them.

Generally, remote communities are well connected even without phone and they know each other on a personal level. One person living nearby to his village heard that two outsiders were enquiring about him. He began doubting the intention of these outsiders and thought that he must have done something wrong, so to be in good faith, he ran to his house and informed the caretaker to leave this place. He told him that two outsiders were enquiring about you. Without giving it a second thought, he disappeared to avoid any kind of conflict in front of his family members.

Later, the Director reached his home and explained the situation to his family members.

So, the caretaker came to his home and understood the situation and agreed to go with them to identify the Rottweiler.

The next morning, they arrived at the airport and took a flight back to country and immediately headed to the kennel to identify the client's Rottweiler's.

The Director, exhausted, both mentally and physically, resigned from the job.

During the demolition process, all the items were tagged except the two dogs

The Family event

One of my cousin's marriage had been fixed. All the family members decided to do the marriage function in their home city because most of the people are known and because of the comfort that comes with one's home city. Accordingly, everything was planned well; the marriage hall was booked, along with the decoration, the food, etc. The 50% advance had also been paid. The entire family was feeling at peace. Everybody had planned to reach home 10 days before. The mother of the bride was in the Middle East and she had come to meet her daughter. The bride, who was in the UK had decided to meet her mother in the Middle East, but finally they both decided to leave together to the home city.

All the arrangement in the home city were made by the uncle, who was managing the entirety of the marriage project.

The mother began to feel a pain in her stomach, which she took painkillers for. Everything was in control.

Then she complained that had been having this kind of pain persistently for the past year. Upon hearing this information, it was decided to go through checkups to know the real reason of the stomach ache. We visited the hospital for various checkups and went through them after necessary registrations. The results were to be received by next day.

The next day, the results came. They changed everything. With only 12 days left for the wedding, the mother had been diagnosed with cancer. The doctor advised us to immediately go to a particular hospital in Delhi for treatment. The focus had shifted from the marriage to the treatment completely.

The next day the mother and the daughter (the would be bride), were flown to reach the hospital.

11 days to the wedding.

The bride- groom's side of the story:

all the arrangements had been made; everything was set.

Most of their relatives were living in different countries. The coordination and booking of tickets had been done much in advance to avoid any kind of last minute hassle.

When they were told about the situation, they were shocked but managed to control the situation.

It was complete chaos and things seemed to be going out of hand.

Everyone's minds were fogged by two thoughts; the sickness of the mother and the possibility that the wedding would be called off.

9 days to the wedding and also the day the mother would be operated on. The predefined arrangements had gone to waste.

The new task was to arrange for a new venue in Delhi. No one had a clue of how it would be done.

From the bridegroom's side they had cancelled their previous tickets and once again booked them for Delhi. So one part was done with. Now the next was to book a good venue and all other arrangements for the wedding. The operation of the mother was successful. Everybody felt relieved. The wedding was planned in the hospital. It was very unusual to discuss both the wedding and the illness at the same time. Suddenly a project manager emerged, in the form of the best friend of bride's sister, who was staying in Delhi at the time.

The project brief was; the wedding had to take place on the same particular predefined date within the available budget. This project manager had to work with a focused mind.

After a lot of research, which involved visiting many possible venues, it was finalized at a fantastic location with all facilities including five star catering. All the family members felt like they were on top of the world. The arrangement for the venue was a complete success, and the mother's health was rapidly improving.

The situation allowed for the project Manager to take the appropriate decision on her own as the entire family was preoccupied with nursing the mother back to health. The decision process was very prompt. In all steps of finalization, everything was decided by the Project Manager herself but keeping the bride's family informed about all decisions to keep them in the loop. Finally, what we can learn that the most important ingredient for any successful project is as below

1. Clarity of Project goal
2. Passion to do from the beginning to end
3. clear and concise communication
4. intelligent transparency during project life cycle
5. honesty towards commitment

Each individual is a project manager -

The project can be any job or any moment of life.

Doctors are also project managers

As The Almighty is above, his creations on earth are busy doing and accomplishing their assigned projects. The purpose of human creation is also part of an enormous project.

Last year on the 8th of January I received a call at 3:00 in the morning from India. It was my elder brother, he was crying uncontrollably, his voice was unstable he told me that our mother is no more. An emptiness dawned upon me, consuming me. I was speechless; My senses, a jumble of emotions. The only thing that made sense was to cry. My two daughters and my wife all woke up and started crying upon hearing the news, attempting, through their own tears, to console me. The most crucial project manager was no more, as in the previous chapter, the relationship between the manager and the project was discussed. I am the project of my mother. My younger brother also called and he was crying along with my sisters. We all were the project of one sole project manager. Ammi (mom) was dealing differently with all the projects, providing varying kinds of support based on the requirement of that particular project. My Father was in a state of shock. He was lost because ammi was managing all the projects inside out. Everyone gathered in Lucknow, bearing witness to the saddest moment of my life. Nobody could ever take the place of my mother.

The rule of nature goes as such; nothing is permanent in this world, anything which comes in existence will disappear one day.

Similarly, a project team manages a project successfully then disappears after handing it over to the end users. As time passed, things slowly returned to normal.

Time can't be stopped and thus everyone must move and bend to its will. All projects have their own respective governance, established by the project manager. This is how sometimes projects seem to run on their own; Someway or the other, everyone begins to learn to work on their own.

After the funeral, we decided to bring my father along to stay with us.

My father was on medication for all possible chronic medical conditions.

The results of his medical tests portrayed a overall balanced review, and the doctors permitted him to travel.

My father ecstatic about the fact that he would be able to spend time with his grand children.

We landed at the Dubai International Airport with him.

Days passed smoothly. To be on the safer side, I took him to the doctor. The doctor was a close friend. I had called him and informed him earlier about my father's arrival and he unhesitatingly said that he would love to meet him. When he saw my father, he checked all his reports and medicines and made a brief report. He advised us to carry out some tests to analyze his present health situation. My brother, who also lives in the UAE, took him to a diagnostic center for blood and urine test.

It was a holiday. At around 5:00pm, my brother's phone started ringing. The number was a landline (generally people don't pick up unknown numbers.) But by fate my brother picked up the phone and through whatever portion of the conversation I could grasp, I made out the word emergency.

The call was from the diagnostic center; the caller said that the reports were not good. The blood urea, creatinine and potassium levels were very high, the potassium level was 8.4

(normal level between 3.5 and 5.0 mEq per liter for adults). I spoke to the doctors. One doctor said that the potassium level truly was elevated to a degree of concern, and that we should consult another doctor. The other doctor said that the value is high, but there should be some other symptoms for cause of alarm. The third Doctor said that the value indicated potassium is 8.4, which is a definite emergency and that the patient must immendiately be admitted in a hospital. I took my father to the emergency room and the doctors took immediate action and sent his blood to lab for a test, along with the performance of an ECG. The ECG was approved of which gave us hope of our father's fast recovery. The only task left was to lower down the elevated values of potassium. He was admitted to the Intensive care unit, where he was kept under thorough observation and treatment. The doctor may be seen as the project manager in this case. He was closely monitoring his project from every aspect.

The next day, the doctor unearthed the real cause of the elevated values and my father was treated accordingly. The potassium level came down to a steady 5.1 which is within the permissible limits. We all were relieved. I have noticed that for the success of any project, the vulnerability of the decision-making stand point must be taken into consideration. Prompt decisions made at the right time assures the success of any project; big or small.

The following principles should be followed

- Staying honest
- showing concern
- compassion
- being confident

Scope creep on the project

I have had innumerate experiences in project management. This versatility of experience that I am lucky enough to be the beholder of creates a different sort of project atmosphere. I once joined a project in the midway of its ongoing; the existing project manager briefed me about the project and warned me that the client was very sensitive about the quality of delivery. I had worked on and completed many projects for a very high profile clientele, involving the development of facilities of varying nature, suchas swimming pools, resorts, luxurious villas and many others. Having this in my mind, I thought of my experience as enough to deal with any sort of project. I arrived at the site of the project;it was a penthouse project. my first impression of it was that it was small in terms of size, but in comparison, the project team was pretty big.

I met with all the site members. The team was very professional, I had observed from their body language. In the site office, everybody was sitting at one place; the client representative, the cost consultant and the main contractor i.e. us. Normally in other projects, each team member sits in a separate room. But this seating style gave me the impression that the project would finish very fast as all the team members would be able to talk face to face.

After about an hour, I was escorted to the site and was shown all the areas. By looking at the overall project, I labeled it an easy project. I then interacted with all the site staff. Everything was seemingly under control. I looked inside the rooms. Mainly on interior projects, three main elements are considered; **floor**, **wall**, and **ceiling**. I observed that all the floors, walls and ceilings were complete except 10% of the final finishes. The client visited the site and looked into it, and requested a lot of changes mostly in all aspects of the project.; even though everything was done based on what the client had previously agreed to. But, there was nothing much to do since it is the client's right to make sure that the project is tailor-made to their liking. The designer started proposing new designs, expecting them to be liked by the client. The whole scenario of the project changed. The completed project trailed back to the initial stages; and now it is even more challenging to superimpose the new concept onto the existing loose ends. The deadlines are also not met due to the fact that the alterations also open another subject of justification for the extension of time. When the client finally snaps out of their daze, they realize that the all the major changes they have requested are destined to take a considerable amount of time. The team onsite was pressurized due to the persistent and radical changes in mostly every area. The real challenge was to maintain a clear justification of the new project time line,

Project organization chart

The project organization chart is one of the most pivotal parts of the project. The organization chart reflects on the positioning of the site management team. When we visit any project, it starts with security and safety induction. Next, is the reception. These are the 2 most important aspects of the organization chart, but in general we do not pay too much attention to them.

In actuality, most projects organization charts are from top to bottom with four to five layers with specified communication lines. In this type of hierarchy, the communication happens in a very filtered; bureaucratic manner. The clear picture of the project will never be displayed. In reports, it may look under control, but hidden issues will remain invisible to address and this may result in them not being sorted out in time.

The project organization must be a flat organization where no hierarchy should be maintained. The communication has to be very clear and straight forward, keeping formalities to a minimum and it should flow from down to up and up to down in order to register all the important points and to perform any necessary corrective actions without delay because the project is in the process of making; where feedbacks nourish the process of making and deliver the best possible end product to client.

Special thanks to Mr. Stephen Konzelmann &
Mr. Anils Nadakkavukaran who inspired me
to learn and understand project management
roles.

∞

Special thanks to Mr. Omar Delwar and Mr. Alan Macready who inspired me to learn and understand many leadership roles.

∞

References

- Kerzner, H., 2009. *Project Management: A System Approach to Planning, Scheduling, and Controlling.* 10th ed. New Jersey: John Wiley & Sons, Inc

- Jack, ribbens(14th feb2000,p 60) simultaneous engineering for new products development, Wiley

- Larry, richman(2nd April 2001,p 1-36) project management step-by-step, AMACOM

- Harold kerzner(2006,p25) project management case studies, john Wiley

- Dariushrafinejad(15june 2007,p 289&293)innovation, product development and commercialization: case studies and key, J. Ross Publishing

- Eugene f.finkin(1988)successful corporate turnarounds, Praeger Paperback

- Agarwal, R., and Prasad, J. (1997). "The Role of Innovation Characteristics and Perceived Voluntariness in the Acceptance of Information Technologies." *Decision Sciences, the Decision Sciences Institute*, 28(3), 557-582.

- Barker, T., and Frolick, M.N. (2003). "ERP Implementation Failure: A Case Study."

Information Systems Management, Auerbach, 20(4),43-49.

- Office of Government Commerce (2005), Managing Successful Projects with PRINCE2 (PRINCE2 Manual), The Stationary Office, (Official PRINCE2 publication), which represented the main inspiration.

- Newman, Pippa (1997), Professionalism in Project Management (Digest No: 1997/373), PRINCE2 [project management method], pages 1-2

- Bradley, Ken (2002), Passing the PRINCE2 examinations, London: The Stationery Office

- Kerzner, Harold (2009) *Project Management: A systems approach to*

Planning, Scheduling and Controlling. New Jersey: John Wiley & Sons, Inc.

- ILX Group (2011). 'PRINCE2 Process Model' http://www.prince2.com/ prince2-process-model.asp. [accessed 3rd December, 2011

- Roger Lever (2009). 'Project Report Format' http://www.articlesfactory.com/ articles/management/project-report-format-example-for-project-status.html [accessed 3rd December, 2011]

- Controlling and Reporting'. http://www.epmbook.com/control.htm [accessed 3rd December, 2011]

- Change Management: http://www.youtube.com/watch?v=MBawvbGokQY &feature=related[accessed 3rd December, 2011]

- Configuration Management: http://www.youtube.com/watch?v=lvVvMmspMYk[accessed 3rd December, 2011]

Printed in the United States
By Bookmasters